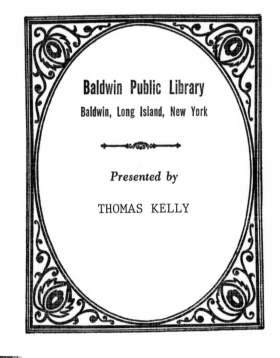

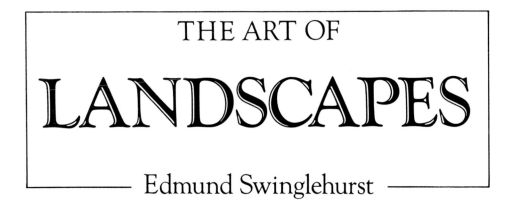

THE ART OF
LANDSCAPES

Edmund Swinglehurst

A Compilation of Works from the
BRIDGEMAN ART LIBRARY

SHOOTING STAR PRESS

Shooting Star Press Inc
230 Fifth Avenue, New York, New York 10001

Landscapes

This edition printed for:
Shooting Star Press, Inc.
230 Fifth Avenue - Suite 1212
New York, NY 10001

ISBN   1 56924 176 7

Printed in Italy

Editor: Alexa Stace
Designer: Robert Mathias

The publishers would like to thank Joanna Hartley
at the Bridgeman Art Library for her invaluable help

LANDSCAPES

Landscape appeared as a background in early Italian paintings, in an elementary form in Giotto's paintings, then in more detail in the work of Mantegna and the Bellini family. It did not become a subject worth painting for its own sake until the Bavarian painter Albrecht Altdorfer made a trip down the Danube early in the 16th century: he was so impressed by the Austrian Alps that he painted them without adding dominating figures to justify the painting.

In the following century landscape became an important part of genre paintings which showed peasant communities as part of their environment. The Bruegels, father and son, were the pioneers of this kind of painting which ignored the grandiose style of most Italian art with its religious and mythological dramas, depicting the life of ordinary people at their everyday activities.

The love of landscape for its own sake was something that many painters felt but, if they were successful and wanted to make a living, could devote little time to. Rubens, after a busy life as court painter, was able to concentrate on landscape painting only after buying his own estate at Het Steen and going into semi-retirement with his young wife, Hélène Fourment. His direct, forceful vision of the countryside brought a new spirit into Dutch landscape painting which flourished in the works of such painters as Hobbema and Ruisdael.

In France landscape continued to have the role of a setting for mythological stories, but the personages of the dramas now played a much smaller role than hitherto. Claude and Poussin both devoted most of the space on their canvases to the landscape itself, Claude taking a romantic view of it with warm atmospheric colours which enveloped feathery trees and Roman buildings and Poussin making structural compositions in which every part of the landscape fitted into a classical framework.

From these Dutch and the French sources there sprang new streams of landscape painting inspiration. In England, Richard Wilson, John Crome and John Sell Cotman of the Norwich School tended to follow the Dutch style; a little later, Constable and Turner found inspiration in Claude, though they created something entirely new from his vision.

Turner, beginning as a classical painter, became a visionary of paint, creating atmospheric paintings of great power; Constable, on the other hand, devoted himself to exploring the truths that lay in the actual matter of nature itself, making endless studies of trees, water, plants and clouds. His paintings took some time to be accepted in England but had a powerful effect on French artists, opening the way to Impressionism.

The Impressionists combined scientific theory about colour with an imitation of the way in which sunlight strikes; they split colours into their components and applied pure colours in small brushstrokes to obtain the effect of shimmering sunshine and shadow.

Cézanne thought this effect too superficial and dedicated himself to a search for the deeper truth of the structure of the countryside by studying the actual form of trees, hills and rocks. This led away from the study of nature into a new aesthetic in which nature became the inspiration but not the guardian of a quintessential truth held in natural objects.

A landscape painting thus became more a panorama of the painter's mind than a depiction of the found truths in a country scene. Picasso, Matisse and their followers did not have much interest in landscape painting; when they did produce a landscape, it was an invented one, as they used nature for their own ends and created a new interpretation of the world about us.

▷ **River Landscape** Jan Bruegel (1568-1625)

Oil on canvas

JAN BRUEGEL was the younger son of the Dutch satirist and landscape painter Pieter Bruegel, nicknamed 'Peasant Bruegel' because of the interest in rural life expressed in his paintings. Like his father, Jan travelled to Italy and knew, but was relatively uninfluenced by, the Italian Renaissance painters. Jan Bruegel's roots, like those of his father, were in the north and he therefore developed a closer affinity with life around him in the Netherlands than with the artificial world of mythological gods and goddesses of Italian paintings. Although Jan Bruegel's still lifes and wonderfully detailed landscapes brought him success in his own time, and the nickname 'Velvet Bruegel', he is best remembered today for work he did in collaboration with Rubens. For this painting Bruegel has taken a typical scene along a Dutch waterway, with a heavily laden boat heading up river while local peasants walk along the river bank heading for the large town in the distance on the right of the painting.

◁ Landscape with a Rainbow
Peter Paul Rubens (1577-1640)

Oil on canvas

WHEN RUBENS MARRIED Hélène Fourment after the death of his first wife Isabelle, he was 53 and Hélène 16. Hélène renewed the painter/diplomat's inspiration and his creative powers. Retiring to his estate at Steen in the Netherlands, he set about developing his latent talent for landscape painting, the subject he had first studied as a young man with the painter Verhaecht. Though he had spent most of his life painting heroic pictures for the Church and the courts of Spain, France and England, at the same time carrying out diplomatic missions for the Spanish Governors of the Netherlands, Rubens had lost none of his feeling for the Netherlands countryside. As this painting shows, Rubens painted with a realism that broke with the classical style and made him a forerunner of Gainsborough, another painter whose talent for painting the country was impeded by the constant demands for his portraits of the high society of his time.

△ **The Storm** Nicholas Poussin (1594-1665)

Oil on canvas

ALTHOUGH THE SUBJECT of this painting is clearly the storm of the title, Poussin does not allow emotional expressionism to upset the cool classicism of the composition. The drama is there – in the buildings lit up by a flash of lightning and in the frightened gestures of the man fleeing from the cart, where two figures gesticulate in terror among the blankets, and in the kneeling carter – but the emotion is seen objectively. The trees, mountains and bushes, though agitated by the storm, are part of the orderly world of the composition which expresses the calm philosophy of the Age of Reason in which Normandy-born Poussin lived.

▽ **Landscape at Dusk** Claude Lorrain (1600-82)

Oil on canvas

The golden glow of an evening sky is characteristic of a painting by the French-born Claude, and is in keeping with the romantic subjects that the painter chose as themes for his landscape paintings. Many of these were of classical themes that Claude had absorbed during visits to Italy, and especially to Rome in 1627, though his style was in the Mannerist tradition of northern artists. Painting four landscapes for Pope Urban VIII helped Claude become well-known, and by his late 30s his reputation as a landscape painter was considerable. He was soon showered with commissions for the 400 or more paintings that are today found in most of the galleries of Europe. Although limited in style and content – he rarely explored nature's other moods as Turner did – Claude created a world of nature which was original and perfect, a setting for the world of the self-contained courts of monarchical Europe.

◁ **Landscape with a Coach** Rembrandt van Rijn (1606-69)

Oil on canvas

REMBRANDT, like his near-contemporary and fellow Dutchman Rubens, was a powerful personality whose paintings have a heroic stature. Both of them chose to concentrate on landscape late in their painting life, having devoted themselves earlier to earning a living by satisfying the demand for their figure compositions and portraits. Unlike Rubens, who was a diplomat and art buyer for the king of Spain, Rembrandt lived solely by his painting, though his wife Saskia (subject of many of his paintings) brought him a large dowry. When his commissions began to decline he became poor and only survived thanks to the support of his son, Titus, and his mistress Hendrickje Stoffels, who had some income of her own. Rembrandt's landscape paintings were inspired, like those of Rubens, by an intense love of his native countryside and have the same dynamic air about them; the romantic air of many of his earlier landscapes had given way, by the 1640s, to a much more deeply-felt emotional response to the subject.

▷ **Extensive Mountain Landscape**
David Teniers the younger (1610-90)

Oil on canvas

DAVID TENIERS was a prolific and successful painter of the genre scenes of peasant life which the Netherlands painters had made famous and which were eagerly collected by English art lovers. He was the son of a Dutch painter of religious pictures and landscapes, also called David. The younger David became the more famous and was eventually Court Painter and Keeper of the Pictures for the Archduke Leopold Wilhelm, Regent of the Netherlands. Teniers's interest in landscape began with the work of Jan Bruegel, though he quickly developed a distinctive style of his own. Teniers chose scenes similar to those of Bruegel and Adriaen Brouwer, but painted them in a lighter and brighter way; he also depicted local life in a more conventional way, which was acceptable to the rich and lordly patrons of the time, such as the Archduke Leopold Wilhelm, the Prince of Orange and the Bishop of Ghent. There was so much demand for his work that Teniers set up a large studio, and many of the 2000 pictures attributed to him today may well include work by his assistants.

◁ **Landscape with Cattle
and Figures**
Albert Cuyp (1620-91)

Oil on canvas

CUYP WAS A MEMBER of a
Dordrecht family of engravers
and painters and, unusually
for his period, devoted himself
largely to the painting of
landscape, though he also
produced some fine portraits
and sea-pieces. He was much
influenced by Italian painters
in the way in which he dealt
with scenery; the whole
countryside of his landscapes is
bathed in a clear light in the
style of Giovanni Bellini.
Cuyp's direct approach to
nature, as displayed in
painting after painting of the
canals, mills and cattle of his
native countryside, had a
considerable effect on English
painters. He was much
admired by Richard Wilson
and John Crome, while
Constable was to comment
on his ability to create a
chiaroscuro effect in essentially
light paintings. Cuyp was lucky
enough to marry a wealthy
woman in 1688, and so he
was able to paint the kind of
pictures that pleased him,
instead of those potential
buyers might want.

△ **Landscape with Village** Jacob Isaakszoon van Ruisdael (1628-82)

Oil on canvas

RUISDAEL CAME FROM a family of landscape painters that included his father, Isaak and his uncle, Salomon. The family lived at Haarlem in Holland and much of his early work was of the surrounding countryside. As a landscape painter, Ruisdael did not earn much money, as this form of art was less in demand than figure compositions and genre scenes; fortunately, he had another source of income, for he practised as a doctor in Amsterdam, and was able to paint as he wished. Ruisdael is considered to be the greatest of the realist landscape painters of Holland and his influence was felt throughout European landscape painting well into the 19th century. His way of handling light and dark areas in a landscape painting was brought to perfection by John Constable over a century later.

△ **Road on the Dyke** Meindert Hobbema (1638-1709)

Oil on canvas

THOUGH THE SKY takes up a large part of the canvas in this painting, the artist has subordinated it to the landscape of trees where cottages can be glimpsed among the foliage and people walk and talk in the cast shadows. The painting is typical of the work of Hobbema, a pupil of Ruisdael. Hobbema was not a success as a painter in his own country and spent much of his adult life assaying wine barrels for the Dutch Excise, a post he obtained through his wife, who was a maid to the Burgomaster of Amsterdam. Discouraged by his failure to sell paintings, Hobbema apparently painted little in later life; but by one of the ironies of fate, he became popular soon after his death. His work became particularly sought after by British collectors following the reigns of William of Orange and Queen Anne when Dutch influence was having an effect on British agriculture and architecture. The intimacy of Hobbema's country scenes, like this one, with its composition divided by the central tree, appealed to English art-lovers, many of whom belonged to the landed gentry of the still largely agricultural Britain.

◁ **Landscape with Watermill** François Boucher (1703-70)

Oil on canvas

BOUCHER, WHO WAS BORN in Paris, began his artistic life as an engraver for the painter Watteau; having won the Prix de Rome of the Academy, he went to study in Italy in 1727. His taste for rococo decorative art drew him towards artists such as Veronese, Rubens and Tiepolo, the last named becoming the main influence on his style. Back in France, he was greatly helped in his career by Madame de Pompadour, mistress of Louis XV and a power behind the throne. She became his friend and patron and sat for her portrait by Boucher several times.

Boucher's success as a painter was due to the way in which he used his fine technique in portraying in delicately decorative style hedonistic scenes which pleased the members of Louis XV's court. (That they also displeased more serious people like Diderot, the encyclopaedist and writer who was critical of such frivolity, did not upset Boucher's career at all.) In this painting Boucher has set aside his usual chubby nudes and painted a simple country scene – though it retains Boucher's typical air of the countryside as a setting for romance.

△ **Mount Snowdon** Richard Wilson (1714-82)

Oil on canvas

RICHARD WILSON'S classical education had a strong influence on his landscape painting, leading him along the same road explored by Poussin. Wilson was, however, a less severe classicist, displaying more than a touch of Claude's romanticism. He began his career as a portrait painter, but turned almost completely to landscape after a long stay in Italy in the early 1750s. This proved to be more satisfying to him as an artist but less financially rewarding. The Italian landscapes he painted on his return to England were less popular with buyers, so he concentrated on English and Welsh views: this one of Mount Snowdon is typical. It beautifully combines a classical approach with a light airiness that foreshadows future English landscape painting.

▷ **Going to Market Early**
Thomas Gainsborough
(1727-88)

Oil on canvas

THOUGH GAINSBOROUGH is known as one of the greatest of English portrait painters, he preferred to think of himself as a landscape painter who, because of the demands of his public, had to spend his life doing portraits of the rich and powerful people of the society of his times. His greatest wish, according to him, was to retire quietly to the country with his viola de gamba and paint country scenes. In his early years as a painter he was an admirer of Dutch painting and his landscapes of Suffolk, his home county, are reminiscent of Ruisdael and Hobbema, particularly the intimate country genre scenes of the latter. Later in his life, Gainsborough became more interested in the paintings of Claude Lorrain, Watteau and Gravelot. Rubens was also an influence at this time, Gainsborough sharing with him a natural talent with the brush which produced the very delicate treatment of the trees and bushes that gave his canvases their translucent glow.

◁ **A Shepherd Playing the Flute While a Peasant Girl Listens** Jean Honoré Fragonard (1732-1806)

Oil on canvas

WHILE DUTCH AND ENGLISH landscape painters of the 18th century were moving towards a greater realism, French painters whose patrons were usually nobility in the enclosed and artificial atmosphere of Versailles and other royal and noble palaces, were indulging in the art of fantasy. Louis XIV, Louis XV, and Louis XVI, in keeping a firm grip on their nobility, encouraged a theme park existence for them. The artists of the period responded, with Boucher painting chubby little sexy nudes and Watteau, Lancret and Fragonard offering scenes of elegant and discreet eroticism. Madame du Barry commissioned Fragonard to paint *The Progress of Love* for her home at Louveciennes, a painting which included the idealized shepherds and nymphs of pre-revolutionary France. This charming picture offers a variation on the basic theme.

▷ **Landscape with a Rainbow**
Joseph Wright of Derby
(1734-97)

Oil on canvas

JOSEPH WRIGHT'S WORK is
known particularly for its light
effects which, like the work of
Caravaggio, make use of the
dramatic illumination which
can be produced by the use of
intensely dark and light areas.
Ruisdael and Hobbema had
already experimented in this
way, but Wright was more
directly influenced by the
Dutch painter van der Neer.
Caravaggio and his followers
had exploited the effect of
candlelight in their genre
paintings and so did Wright in
his paintings of interiors; but
in landscapes he made use of
moonlight or other natural
phenomena, such as the
rainbow in this painting. Apart
from visits to London, Bath
and Italy, Wright spent most of
his working life in his native
town, Derby, where he found
many admirers and patrons
who encouraged him to paint
pictures with a scientific or
industrial theme, such as his
Experiment with an Air Pump,
which is in the Tate Gallery in
London.

▷ **Wooded River Landscape with Figures and Cattle**
Alexander Nasmyth (1758-1840)

Oil on canvas

THE INFLUENCE OF DUTCH painters is clearly evident in the work of Edinburgh-born Alexander Nasmyth, one of a Scottish family of portrait and landscape painters. Nasmyth went to Italy in 1782, where he studied the Renaissance painters and the work of other landscape painters of the 18th century. After a period as a pupil of Alan Ramsay, the famous Scottish portrait painter, Nasmyth set himself up in Edinburgh as a portrait painter, too. Among his friends was the poet Robbie Burns, whose portrait in the Scottish National Gallery is one of Nasmyth's best-known works. In later life, Nasmyth turned more to the painting of landscapes: this one is a typical example. The stylized trees are typical of the period as are the people in this genre scene of country life, all of which show Dutch influence.

△ **Windy Day** George Morland (1763-1804)

Oil on canvas

THE SON OF A PAINTER, Henry Morland, and gifted enough to have his work exhibited at the Royal Academy when he was only 10, George Morland, like Turner, became very well known through the sale of engravings of his work, which were produced plentifully and cheaply by William Ward. His success was also due in part to the fact that he painted in a familiar, picturesque style derived from Dutch painters like Teniers and Brouwer. In *Windy Day* he includes such typical genre touches as a peasant and his wife returning from market and a horse and cart following. Though a successful painter, Morland lived well beyond his means and was eventually arrested and put in the King's Bench Prison for debt. While there, he produced a large number of work of doubtful quality, to pay off his debts. He died in prison and his reputation as an artist died with him.

▷ **Clearing in the Forest**
Caspar David Friedrich
(1774-1840)

Oil

FRIEDRICH WAS A GERMAN painter with an unusual imagination and belongs to the world of landscape painters like Jan Bruegel and Samuel Palmer as an interpreter of the sub-world of nature rather than a painter of reality. He was very much in the tradition of European Romantics. Friedrich was one of the few painters of his time who did not go to Italy to study the Renaissance masters. He thus escaped their powerful influence and was able to develop his own original style in which nature is full of mystery and a pagan atmosphere where gods, goblins, and other strange Nordic spirits could reside. In this painting, the other-worldly atmosphere is enhanced by the scene's being lit by moonlight. Like most unusual artists, Friedrich, who was trained in Copenhagen and spent most of his working life in Dresden, was little known until more recent and more tolerant times.

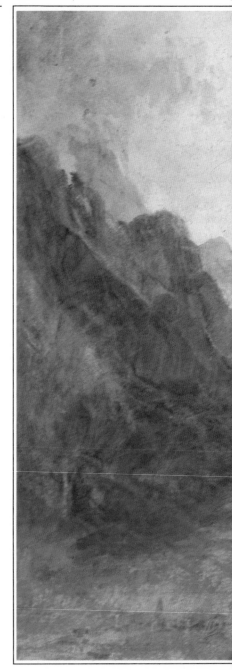

▷ **View Along an Alpine Valley, possibly the Val d'Aosta**
J. M. W. Turner (1775-1851)

Watercolour

THE MOST DRAMATIC and imaginative of landscape painters had a long early career as a painter of carefully worked classical scenes based on stories of Greece and Rome. Since this was what the public wanted and what the Royal Academy accepted, Turner was soon elected as a professor and then a member of the Royal Academy. After his first visit to the Continent, during which he made hundreds of sketches which he later turned into paintings, Turner's style began to change, becoming more fluid and romantic. In this study of an Alpine valley, made on his first trip abroad in 1802, he has handled the watercolour with immense confidence. He started his paintings with broad washes on which he later worked with great care with a fine brush for the final details of accent and tone. Turner's romanticism often made him exaggerate the scale of mountains, valleys and buildings, a habit which accorded with the public's own feelings about the little known natural phenomena of the seas and mountains of Europe.

◁ **Landscape with Hill and Clouds (probably Yorkshire)**
Thomas Girtin (1775-1802)

Watercolour

IN HIS SHORT LIFE Thomas Girtin showed a great talent for innovation which, given time, might have equalled that of his friend Turner. Like the famous painter, he started his career copying drawings, especially those of Canaletto. His favourite media was watercolour, which he turned from what had been traditionally a colouring of drawing into freely handled colour washes which glow with colour and translucency. Turner was to develop this technique into a revolutionary way of using colour and tone, with hardly any reference to the drawing of a picture. Girtin achieved his effect by using an absorbent cartridge paper which allowed for great fluidity in the paint washes and a flexibility in forms, as one can see in this painting. Girtin's finest landscapes were painted in the north of England and in France, where he went in the last year of his life, seeking relief from tuberculosis which was to kill him.

▷ A Sluice, perhaps on the Stour
John Constable (1776-1837)

Oil

JOHN CONSTABLE was born in Suffolk and was deeply influenced by his response to the countryside of the county. To him, a landscape was a real and living thing, not merely a background to a painting or the setting for a classical scene. He felt deeply about the actual matter of nature – here, the gnarled and twisted trees, the muddy banks of the river (probably the Suffolk Stour), the rotting boards at the locks and sluice-gates, the water itself, sometimes crisp and lively and at other times slow and muddy. All this was the flesh and blood of the countryside and Constable spent many hours looking at it and meditating on its implications for art. He did not turn out the kind of paintings that the general public or the Royal Academy found acceptable, and it was some time before he was elected a member of the R.A. In Paris, however, where he exhibited the *Haywain,* today one of his best-known works, he had an encouraging success with other painters, in particular Delacroix, and he opened up avenues of thought in French painting which led to the nature paintings of the Impressionists.

◁ **The Mill** John Sell Cotman (1782-1842)

Watercolour

COTMAN, ALONG WITH CROME, Stannard and others, was one of the members of the Norwich School of English painting. Because of the long-standing links between East Anglia and the Netherlands, there was a good deal of Dutch influence on the Norwich painters, both as regards style and subject matter. Cotman, who was the outstanding artist of the school, particularly in watercolour, was an engraver as well as a painter. He made 60 plates for the *Architectural Antiquities of Norfolk*, a commission which led to other work, such as *Architectural Antiquities of Normandy*. In the end his success with engraving took up more and more of his time, at a cost to his painting, although his position as drawing master of King's College, London – a post Turner helped him obtain – enabled him to pass on some of his understanding of painting and drawing to others.

◁ **Landscape** David Cox (1783-1859)

Watercolour

DAVID COX was a contemporary of Turner and Constable, who first exhibited at the Royal Academy in 1805. He painted mostly in watercolour, with most of his income being derived from teaching his skill and writing about it, notably in a book called *Treatise on Landscape Painting and Effect in Watercolours* (1813-14). He visited Holland, Belgium and France to study paintings in the museums, but did not get to Italy. In fact, the main influence on his work was the landscape of North Wales, especially that around Bettws-y-Coed, which he visited almost every autumn. His style is therefore very much in a northern European tradition, uninfluenced by Italian painting. His facility and the authority with which he handled paint, applying it with a broad, free brushstroke, is not unlike Constable's. From the early 1840s Cox also worked in oil, having taken lessons in oil painting quite late in life, but his watercolours are the more prized.

▷ Avray Village Showing the Cabassud Houses
Jean Baptiste Corot (1796-1875)

Oil on canvas

IT WAS DURING a two-year stay in Rome in the mid-1820s that Corot, who had already had training in the studios of landscape painters, began to paint in the open air, developing his perception of the tonal values of a landscape. By direct observation he learned how to give structure to his paintings and create a sense of space and distance. The clear air of the Campania also impelled him to lighten his palette and to produce paintings full of freshness and light. Later on in life, his painting became more atmospheric and sentimental and, as a consequence, extremely popular – but in this picture of Avray, a village near Paris, there is a clarity and objectivity that puts it between the work of Poussin and Cézanne and shows Corot as a precursor of the liberated art of the end of the century.

▷ **Landscape** Sir Edwin Landseer (1802-73)

Oil on canvas

LANDSEER FIRST EXHIBITED at the Royal Academy at the age of 12. He went on to enjoy a brilliant career as a painter of animals with quasi-human sentimental expressions. Many of his paintings, such as *The Monarch of the Glen* and *The Stag at Bay,* were reproduced as engravings by his brother Thomas and sold to thousands of public houses and private homes throughout Victorian England. The highlands of Scotland attracted him and some of his finest paintings have highland themes. It was probably there that he painted this unidentified landscape, which reveals his talent for handling paint and flair for reproducing nature realistically. Landseer was knighted by an admiring Queen Victoria in 1850, having refused the honour in 1842. His best-known works are not paintings, but the lions that sit at the foot of Nelson's column in Trafalgar Square, London.

◁ **The Shadowy Stream**
Samuel Palmer (1805-81)

Oil on canvas

LIKE HIS MENTOR and friend
William Blake, Samuel Palmer
was more concerned with the
inner life than apparent
reality. Meeting Blake, the
visionary poet and artist, in
1824 had a powerful effect on
the young Palmer; the work of
his 'Shoreham period' from
1826-35, when he was living
on the south coast of England,
was the most interesting of his
life, achieving a fine balance
between reality and the
imaginative mysticism that
mark Blake's poetry. In *The
Shadowy Stream* a shepherd
plays a pipe to a young
woman as the setting sun lights
up the trees in a mysterious
glow against a sky of neatly
striated clouds, the whole
atmosphere being reminiscent
of a Blake poem. Palmer
himself described his painting
of this period as being 'the
product of a primitive and
infantile feeling'.

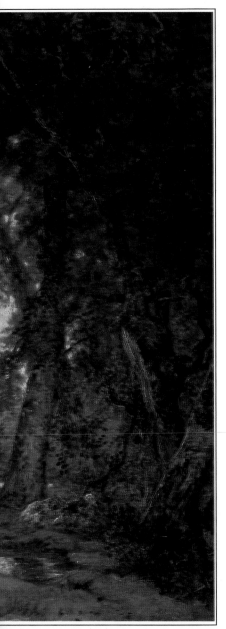

◁ **The Forest at Fontainebleau**
Theodore Rousseau 1812-67

Oil on canvas

ROUSSEAU WAS BORN IN PARIS, where he studied the old masters in the Louvre. He became a principal member of the Barbizon School, a group of painters, including Millet and Diaz, who settled in the village of Barbizon, in the forest of Fontainebleau. The aim was to get away from the stiff, academic style of landscape painting and produce something more rooted in reality. But they were living in a romantic era, and the country people they painted are seen today as idealized, unlike the peasants that van Gogh, for example, painted later. The actual countryside they painted, on the other hand, has much of the reality of a Constable interpretation, as the treatment of trees and marshy ground in this painting demonstrates.

Porto Tre Scoglie, Albania 1862 Edward Lear (1812-88)

▷ *Overleaf pages 48-49*

Watercolour

THE FAMOUS WRITER of limericks and 'nonsense rhymes' would far rather have made his reputation with the paintings to which he devoted his life. Lear began his artistic career as a painter of birds and then turned to topography in oil and watercolours. During his lifetime English people were becoming ubiquitous travellers and Lear's scenes of his own travels around the Mediterranean and Middle East found a ready market. In Lear's work there is an echo of the early work of Turner, whom he had met while studying at the Royal Academy, but his imagination did not stretch as far as the painter who was later to upset so many critics. This painting was made at Porto Tre Scoglie (the port of the three reefs) in Albania, on one of his many painting trips abroad. Many of his best landscapes were done in Italy and Greece.

◁ **Spring** Charles Francois Daubigny (1817-78)

Oil on canvas

A FRENCH LANDSCAPE PAINTER, Daubigny was a friend of Corot and shared with him an enthusiasm for painting direct from nature. His travels abroad took him to England, where he discovered Constable, and he was sufficiently influenced by him to begin to break away from the conventional French Academy style and like Courbet, another French contemporary, strike out on a path that would eventually lead to the Impressionists. Daubigny became, in fact, a friend of the young Monet and therefore was a link between the Barbizon School of painters, by whom he was greatly influenced, and the Impressionists. The lightness of his touch in this delightful painting (done in 1857) especially in the handling of the trees in blossom, is very close to the work Monet and his friends would be producing a decade or so later.

▽ **The Oak of Flagey, called Vercingetorix** Gustave Courbet (1819-77)

Oil on canvas

THE SPLENDID OAK TREE which dominates this picture was named after the heroic Gaul, Vercingetorix, who defied the Roman armies and even inflicted defeat on Julius Caesar before he was finally captured and imprisoned. He was the kind of character who would have appealed to Courbet, a violent non-conformist, often in trouble with the authorities. His naturally rebellious spirit drove him to paint nature directly with the same fervour as Constable, though with less technical care. The result is that many of his paintings have suffered material deterioration. In this painting he has applied the paint with a passionate intensity that gives the tree a heroic character and a sense of the eternity of nature – in contrast with the brief life of individual animals, represented here by the rabbit chased by a dog.

△ **Mountainous Landscape** John Ruskin (1819-1900)

Watercolour

THE MOST INFLUENTIAL English art critic of the second half of the 19th century was also a draughtsman of considerable talent. As one might expect, given Ruskin's well-known interest in architecture, much of his work was dominated by buildings, but he also had a keen interest in nature, which he tended to view with the same objectivity as he gave to stone and mortar. In his later years he lived in the Lake District and this unidentified watercolour drawing may be a view in the vicinity of Coniston Water, where his house, Brantwood, was situated. It is a careful topographical study in which accuracy is more important than imagination, and the figures give scale to the composition. Much of his work is kept at Oxford University, where he was the first Slade Professor of Fine Art, and at Bembridge School, Isle of Wight.

◁ **Hillside at Etretat**
George Inness (1825-94)

Oil on canvas

INNESS WAS AN AMERICAN who did the routine Grand Tour for painters of his period by studying in Rome and Florence and then settling in Paris. Here, he was able to shake free to some extent from the influence of the Italians by getting to know the Barbizon School of painters at Fontainebleau. Under their influence he began to identify with the idea that landscape painting should be a straightforward representation of nature and country life without any subjective distortion – an impossible aim, as all art is inevitably seen through the artist's own personality. In this painting, Inness has set out to paint a shepherdess and her flock without the romanticism that was usually attached to such a theme. In the background are the white cliffs of Etretat in Normandy, which Monet would later also make the subject of numerous paintings.

▷ **The Banks of the Oise, near Pontoise. Cloudy Weather**
Camille Pissarro (1831-1903)

Oil on canvas

PISSARRO, who was a friend of Courbet and Manet, was one of a group of young French artists who developed the idea of painting in the open air and putting the colour down in broken brushstrokes in order to imitate the effect of sunshine on landscape. This technique, which became known as Impressionism, was seized on by other young painters, including Monet and Sisley, who often visited Pissarro. Of them all Pissarro and Sisley were the most consistent in their use of the Impressionist style. Like most innovative painters, Pissarro sold very few works in his lifetime and lived in poverty, but continued to work assiduously. Much of his work remains, even though about 300 of his paintings were destroyed by German soldiers, who used them as duckboards during the German invasion and siege of Paris in 1870. In this winter painting one can appreciate how the Impressionist technique makes even a bleak scene wonderful.

▷ The Cliffs of the Upper Colorado, Wyoming Territory
Thomas Moran (1837-1926)

Oil

AMERICAN 19TH-CENTURY landscape painters, most of whom studied in Paris, were very much influenced by the European tradition. Moran, who was actually born in England, used techniques derived from Impressionism to paint scenes that were very unlike European ones. His theme was the opening up of the American West. In this painting he has included a band of Indians trekking past a background of massive mesetas. Like Poussin, he makes the figures small in relation to nature, perhaps to show that man is helpless against natural forces. The Western theme served Moran well; Congress bought two of his paintings for $10,000.

◁ **Countryside in Provence** Paul Cézanne (1838-1906)

Watercolour

CÉZANNE IS REGARDED as the father of modern art because his painting technique, which consisted of a meticulous analysis of the structure of objects, led to Cubism: a development of Cézanne's technique by Picasso and Braque. Having studied Impressionism closely, Cézanne decided that it lacked the formal structure that he sought in representing reality. Leaving Paris and his Impressionist friends, Cézanne returned to Aix-en-Provence, where his family lived. Working in the warm, clear light of the south of France, he began to develop the very individual style that will always be associated with his work. His strong feeling for an ordered classicism made him an admirer of Poussin whom he wanted to emulate, but working directly from nature. With this end in view, he set himself to study the structure of things, whether they were pots and apples or mountains and trees. In doing so he was reflecting 20th-century society's scientific and objective view of the world. At first, his art was rejected by the public, but he later came to be seen as the prophet of modern art. In this watercolour which appears so simple at first glance, Cézanne has constructed a solid landscape, out of planes of colour chosen after much thought, to create a three-dimensional world describing the Provencal countryside before him.

△ **Lady's Cove and Langland Bay** Alfred Sisley (1839-99)

Oil on canvas

SISLEY APPROACH TO NATURE was quiet and contemplative, unlike Monet's whose subjects included the stormy coastline seas of France. Sisley's quiet approach, typified by this peaceful Welsh coastal scene painted in 1897, did not attract much attention and, unlike other Impressionists, he did not become rich. The original and personal quality of his vision came to be appreciated later especially in England, the home of his parents, though he was born in Paris. Sent to England at 18 to learn his father's business, he discovered Constable and Turner and returned to Paris determined to become a painter. There, at Gleyre's studio, he met young artists like Renoir and Monet who were destined to become leaders of Impressionism and he joined their circle. Like them, he painted the villages of the Seine, near Paris. He also painted the Thames in its quieter reaches up-river. Today, Sisley, Monet and Pissarro are regarded as the painters most dedicated to the ideas that created the Impressionist era of painting.

△ **The Small Haystacks** Claude Monet (1840-1926)

Oil on canvas

MONET'S INTRODUCTION to the idea of painting direct from nature, a practice already introduced to some extent by Constable and the Barbizon School painters, came through Eugène Boudin whom he met while living with his family in Le Havre. Enthused by the idea of taking his easel into the open and completing a painting face to face with his subject, Monet began a series of journeys to places that appealed to him in order to produce a batch of work on each subject. He did this at Belle Ile on the west coast of France, at Etretat and on the French and Italian Rivieras. Later, as he concentrated on exploring the relationship between light and colour, he chose to work with subjects nearer home, having many canvases in work at the same time. Thus came about the great series of his later life: poplars, Rouen Cathedral, and the haystacks near his home, all of them painted in all seasons and at different times of the day. The grand culmination of his life's work was the series of paintings based on the garden he had planned and planted at Giverny.

△ **Landscape with Green Corn** Vincent van Gogh (1853-90)

Oil on canvas

VAN GOGH'S LANDSCAPES are so original and personal that it is difficult to believe that he was, in fact, strongly influenced by intellectual ideas current among the artists he had worked with while studying in Paris. His many letters to his brother Theo reveal that he thought a great deal about his painting, though he had the ability to throw off the inhibiting tethers of reason and paint what he felt. His dual nature made life stressful for him and led to frequent bouts of madness: during one of these he cut off his ear after quarrelling with Gauguin, with whom he had been staying at Arles. From Arles, Van Gogh went voluntarily to a lunatic asylum at Saint-Rémy en Provence. It was at Saint-Rémy that van Gogh painted many of his most famous landscapes, his canvases covered in great swirls of colour as he sought to set down the great skies, wind-tossed cypresses and spreading horizons of the south of France. This picture of corn ripening in a field was done at Saint-Rémy in June 1889, during a period of great artistic activity.

▷ **In the Forest at Pontaubert**
George Pierre Seurat
(1859-91)

Oil on canvas

MANY THEORIES of modern art,
while helping to destroy the
slavish following of old
traditions, were often carried
to rational conclusions which
became dead-ends. Pointillism,
or Divisionism, was one of
those theories, with many
passionate adherents for a
while. Seurat, Signac, Camoin
and Cross were all faithful to
the Divisionist idea, which
carried forward the
Impressionist principles of
broken colour by breaking the
colour into its primary
components and putting it
down on canvas in small dots.
In the end, the small dots
tended to cancel out the
strength of the colour; in
response to this, the Post-
Impressionists began to use
large splashes of pure colour.
In this painting in the forest at
Pontaubert near Avalon in
Burgundy, Seurat's technique
has described accurately the
effect of light on the trunks of
the silver birches and
penetrating the dark
undergrowth beyond.

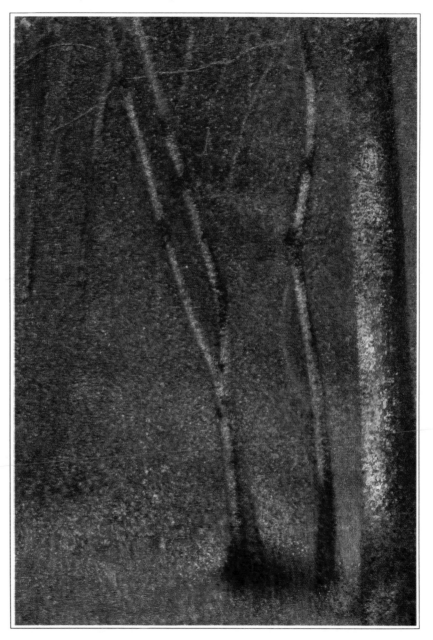

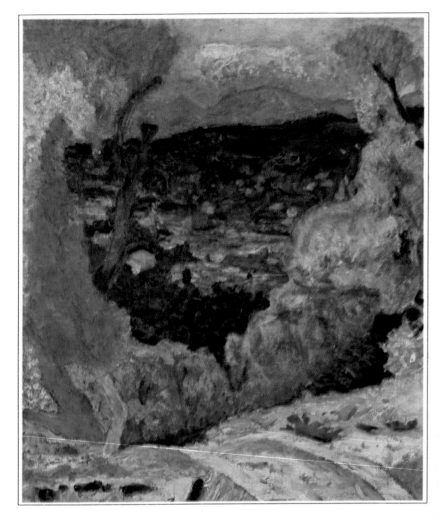

◁ **Southern Setting: Le Cannet** Pierre Bonnard (1867-1947)

Oil on canvas

AS AN ARTIST, Bonnard's feeling for colour was the result of the liberating effect of the Fauve movement. In his search for colour he moved to the south of France in 1908 and lived at Le Cannet, then a small village on the slopes of the hills behind Cannes. This painting of Le Cannet and its surrounding hills was done in the late 1920s. Bonnard used colour as large patches, interacting in brilliant harmony or contrast. Most of Bonnard's subjects were close to home, either in his garden or indoors, where his patient wife Marthe was his model throughout her life. His style of painting, also adopted by Vuillard, with whom he shared a studio for a time, came to be called 'Intimisme', because of the domesticity of its subject matter.

▷ **Landscape in Provence**
Matthew Smith (1879-1959)

Oil on canvas

THE USE OF STRONG COLOUR has never been natural to English painters, brought up under cool skies and pallid sunshine. Halifax-born Matthew Smith is one of the exceptions. Having studied at the Slade School in London, his interest in colour grew out of a visit to Paris in 1910 when he met Matisse and became fascinated by the short-lived Fauve movement whose members were experimenting with violent colour contrasts. Smith's flower and nude subjects and his landscapes, many painted in Provence, gave him ample scope for the creation of powerful and sensual paintings which many found more French than English in feeling.

◁ **A Provençal Landscape**
Vanessa Bell (1879-1961)

Oil

VANESSA BELL was one of the Bloomsbury Group, a community of writers and artists which included her sister Virginia Woolf, Roger Fry and Duncan Grant. The group introduced to England the new ideas about painting which were becoming accepted on the Continent at the turn of the century but which the British public and most art critics rejected. Vanessa Bell was very much influenced by Cézanne, but attempted to combine his technique of painting in broad planes of colour with the tight drawing that was considered technically essential in England. She therefore did not achieve in her work the breadth and strength of the master of Aix. In her later work she became more abstract and worked with Roger Fry in the Omega workshops which were trying to introduce new design ideas into England. This landscape was painted in the south of France in 1928.

△ **Collioure** André Derain (1880-1954)

Oil

DERAIN HAD A NATURAL TALENT for colour and, with Henri Matisse, was one of the short-lived group of painters known as Fauves (wild animals) because of the way they painted. The wild, free-for-all painting style of the Fauves was an attempt to break away from the conventions of Impressionism and it did, in fact, liberate colour just as Cubism liberated drawing. In this painting of the harbour at the fishing village of Collioure on the French-Spanish border, Derain has used pure and contrasting primary colours to give the maximum brilliance to the painting and thus represent the blazing Mediterranean sunshine. The Fauve movement lasted long enough to achieve its effect before its followers moved on to a more formal kind of art. Derain himself returned to a more conventional academic style and, like his Italian contemporary, Giorgio de' Chirico, deserted the idea of modern art altogether.

▷ **The Chateau, La Roche Guyon** Georges Braque (1882-1963)

Oil

BRAQUE AND PICASSO were the founders of the Cubist movement, which set out to examine the structure of the real world in ever greater detail. In this painting done at La Roche Guyon in the valley of the Seine, a popular rendezvous for the Impressionists, Braque turned the hill and the castle into a Cubist exercise, separating out all the planes of the scene before him and then flattening them in order to create a two-dimensional composition. This severe style was a reaction to the coloured mists and dots of the Impressionists and to the colour explosions of the Fauves. In the end, Cubism was not the answer to the dilemma of what a painting should be, either. Braque continued to develop a style called 'Synthetic Cubism' which used the cubist technique in a much freer way and with a closer relationship to the objects painted.

◁ **Vimy Ridge**
Paul Nash (1889-1946)

Oil

LONDON-BORN NASH was brought up in Buckinghamshire, a county of rolling hills marked by woods and the chequerboard fields of a centuries-old farming culture. Images from such landscapes were to show up again and again in his art, which demonstrated a great feel for the geometrical order which Nash perceived as underlying nature. By his mid-twenties his reputation was such that he was appointed an official war artist. Vimy Ridge, a grim landscape of the trenches of northern France, is typical of his work at this time, in which scenes of devastation were given a certain optimism by the sensation of rebirth that lay underneath. Later his landscapes took on a mystical quality, with elements of abstraction and surrealism, as the artist meditated on the cyclical relation between life and death, planting and harvest.

▷ **Stone City, 1930** Grant Wood (1892-1942)

Oil

GRANT WOOD was a painter of the between-the-wars period who used the modern art ideas of Europe to construct stylized views of the landscapes of the Eastern United States. He had much in common with English artists like Ravilious and Nevinson, though he also had a primitive simplicity that went back to early Dutch paintings but was at the same time unmistakably American. Although this landscape, painted in 1930, is cool, there is a feeling that the artist cared deeply about the scene, with its little buildings, windmill and bridge, as if they somehow represent a vision of an idealized America unspoiled by industry.

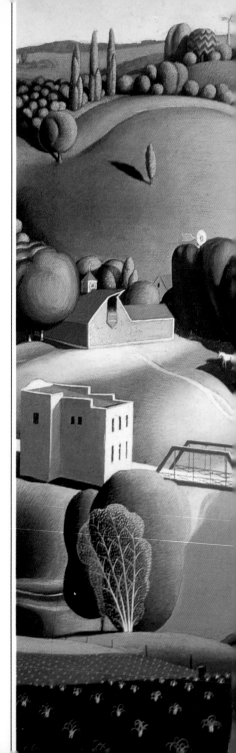

◁ **Dodges Ridge, 1947** Andrew Wyeth (1917-)

Egg tempera on fiber board

THIS BLEAK WINDSWEPT painting of 1947 seems to sum up Andrew Wyeth's feelings about America after the Great Depression and World War II. Like many other artists of the period, Wyeth seems pessimistic about his country, which is apparently failing to live up to its early promise. Trying to escape from such gloomy visions, many artists looked for inspiration in the countryside, seeking nostalgically for grass-root links with the present in the simple, homespun beliefs of the past. Like other American artists of the period, Wyeth was not in tune with the more radical departures taking place in European and East Coast American art, and tended to fall back on traditional techniques.

◁ **Sandy Path**
C. R. W. Nevinson
(1899-1946)

Oil

CHRISTOPHER NEVINSON, the son of a war correspondent and journalist, started off his painting career at the Slade School in London and in Paris. He was at first a follower of Futurism, whose leader, the Italian Marinetti, believed that a racing motor car was more beautiful than the Victory of Samothrace. Nevinson became well known as an official war artist during the First World War. In this painting there is some of the bleakness of his paintings of the battlefields of northern France. The style is traditional English but also reminiscent of earlier European artists like Corot and Jongkind. There is also a trace of Cézanne in the mounds of earth in the foreground which look like a North Downs location. The painting is typical of the work of many English artists of the period who, though they had studied the work of contemporary European painters, were reluctant to be equally experimental.

▷ **Sun Setting Between Hills, 1937** Graham Sutherland (1903-80)

Oil

THERE IS AN AFFINITY between this landscape and the romantic visionary work of Samuel Palmer and Blake. Sutherland, a romantic, was trying to use nature to express philosophical and even mystical ideas. In the landscapes he painted, mostly in Wales, there are thorn and thistle shapes which seem to imply that life is a vale of tears whose tragedy is symbolized by the Crucifixion. When Coventry Cathedral was rebuilt after its wartime destruction Sutherland was commissioned to design a great altar tapestry which also embodies these symbols. It is regarded as one of his most important works. Sutherland was also a notably honest portrait painter, his subjects including such well-known figures as Lord Beaverbrook, Somerset Maugham, Helena Rubenstein and Winston Churchill. Churchill's wife, Clementine, disliked Sutherland's portrait of her aging husband so much that she destroyed it.

▷ **Snowdonia No.1, 1971**
Edward Burra (1905-76)

Oil

THE ENGLISH 19TH-CENTURY
traditional approach to
landscape continued into the
20th century, for some while
resisting the influence of the
Impressionists. The new ideas
eventually helped painters to
break away from tradition and
to express themselves in an
original manner. Burra was
separated from art movements
by his solitary life on the South
Coast of England, developing
a surrealist genre urban scene.
In this painting he gave
Snowdon a new look,
deserting the Turner and
Richard Wilson approach to
give it a naive and perhaps
slightly cubist air, which is
totally original and has the
genuine eccentricity of such
English painters as Palmer and
Blake.

◁ **Trendine, Cornwall, December 1947** Ben Nicholson (1894-1980)

Oil

AN ABSTRACT ARTIST with an international reputation, Nicholson was born in Denham, Buckinghamshire. Although much of his work was purely geometrical, ordinary still-life objects and landscapes often formed the starting-point of his paintings, as in this wintertime study. His delicate sense of colour and elegance of composition is evident here in his depiction of the group of buildings making up the small village, and the hilly, field-marked land beyond leading towards a dark sea. There is some evidence here of the influence of Mondrain and de Stijl. For some years Nicholson lived in Switzerland, but later he returned to Cornwall, where he and his wife, the sculptor Barbara Hepworth, were leading figures in the St Ives group of artists.

ACKNOWLEDGEMENTS

The Publisher would like to thank the following for their kind permission to reproduce the paintings in this book:

Bridgeman Art Library, London/Ackerman and Johnson Ltd, London 30; /**Agnew & Sons, London** 38-39, 48-49; /**Atkinson Art Gallery, Southport, Lancs** 69; /**Bonhams, London** 65, 66; /**Beit Collection, Co. Wicklow, Ireland** 21; /**Bowes Museum, Co. Museum** 22-23; /**British Museum, London** 34-35; /**Castle Museum, Norwich** 24; /**Christie's, London** 28-29, 32-33, 61; /**City Museum and Art Gallery, Stoke-on-Trent** 74; /**Dulwich Picture Gallery, London** 18-19; /**Gavin Graham Gallery, London** 16-17; /**Giraudon/Derby Museum & Art Gallery** 27; /**Giraudon/Musée des Beaux-Arts, Rouen** 12; /**Giraudon/Louvre, Paris** 26, 40-41, 50-51; /**Giraudon/Musée d'Orsay, Paris** 55; /**Giraudon/Musée National d'Art Moderne, Paris** 64; /**Hermitage, St Petersburg** 10-11, 13; /**Joslyn Museum, Omaha** 70-71; /**Kenwood House, London** 25; /**Kunsthaus, Zurich** 58-59; /**Lefevre Gallery, London** 76-77; /**Louvre, Paris** 67; /**Moderna Museet, Stockholm** 68; /**National Gallery, London** 62; /**National Museum of American Art, Smithsonian Inst.** cover, 72-73; /**Neue Galerie, Linz** 31; /**Narodni Galerie, Prague** 62; /**Pennsylvania Academy of Fine Arts, Philadelphia** 52; /**Phillips Collection, Washington D.C.** 78; /**Private Collection** 54, 60, 63, 75; /**Roy Miles Gallery, 29 Bruton Street, London W1** 8-9, 42-43; /**Victoria and Albert Museum** 36, 37, 44-45, 53; /**Wallace Collection, London** 14-15, 20, 46-47.

Vimy Ridge – Paul Nash is reproduced by permission of the Paul Nash Trust.